TRIVIA BOOK WITH ANSWERS

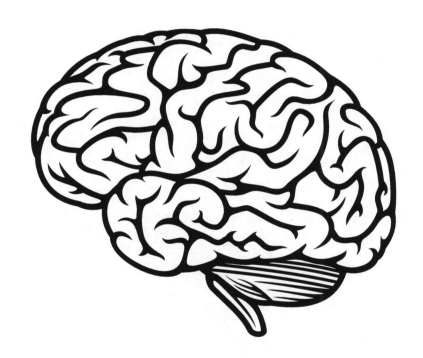

400 Challenging Multiple

Choice Questions !

Thanks for purchasing this book

We hope enjoy it . We put a lot of effort on this book.

All Feedback on amazon is greatly appreciated

SECTION 1

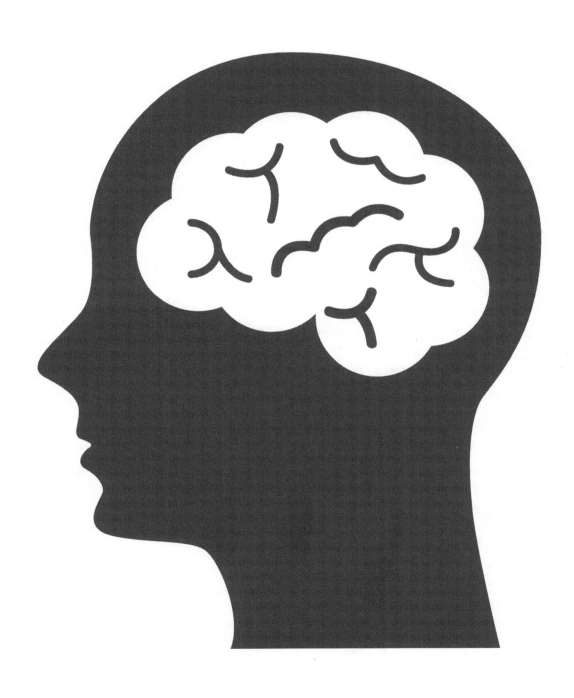

1. Which is the largest living animal on earth?

    A. blue whale
    B. elephant
    C. humpback whale
    D. whale shark

2. When a people are frightened their ears produce more of what?

    A. Earwax
    B. Sweat
    C. Ringing sounds
    D. White blood cells

3. Which type of infection could be treated with antibiotics?

    A. bacterial infection
    B. common cold
    C. fungal infection
    D. viral infection

4. New York City comprises how many boroughs?

    A. 4
    B. 6
    C. 3
    D. 5

5. The aardvark is native to which continent?

    A. Asia
    B. South America
    C. Oceania
    D. Africa

6. Which Dutch artist painted Girl with a Pearl Earring?

    A. Rembrandt
    B. Mondrian
    C. Vermeer
    D. Bosch

7. What happened in the Soviet Union from 1933-1934?

    A. Famine
    B. War
    C. Uprising
    D. Political conflicts

8. What was Toyota's first popular hybrid car called?

    A. Yaris
    B. Matrix
    C. Prius
    D. Camry

9. What of these animals is not an amphibian?

    A. eel
    B. frog
    C. salamander
    D. toad

10. Tim Berners-Lee is credited with the invention of what?

    A. computer
    B. telephone
    C. telescope
    D. World Wide Web

11. What is a baby goat called?

    A. A kid
    B. A pup
    C. A child
    D. A goatling

12. Which country is known as the Land of White Elephant?

    A. India
    B. Thailand
    C. Cambodia
    D. Vietnam

13. Which US state is also called the Aloha State?

    A. Hawaii

    B. Arizona

    C. Colorado

    D. Delaware

14. What percentage of all species on earth are insects?

    A. 10%

    B. 25%

    C. 50%

    D. 80%

15. Where do kiwi fruits originally come from?

    A. Taiwan

    B. Vietnam

    C. China

    D. India

16. How did Anne Frank receive her diary?

    A. Birthday gift

    B. found it

    C. stole it

    D. bought it herself

17. What is the driest continent?

    A. Antartica

    B. Africa

    C. Arctic

    D. Australia

18. How old was Marie Antoinette when she married?

    A. 14

    B. 13

    C. 19

    D. 21

19. What is the capital of Australia?

    A. Sydney

    B. Canberra

    C. Melbourne

    D. Brisbane

20. How many countries have names that end in -stan?

    A. 10

    B. 5

    C. 8

    D. 7

21. Which country is the largest rice producer?

    A. India
    B. China
    C. Israel
    D. Thailand

22. What was the first fruit that was eaten on the moon?

    A. Apple
    B. Plum
    C. Melon
    D. Peach

23. In which European city would you find Orly airport?

    A. Amsterdam
    B. Zurich
    C. Berlin
    D. Paris

24. Who claimed he could drive away the devil with a fart?

    A. Pope Pius X
    B. King Louis IX
    C. Martin Luther
    D. Napoleon

25. What was the ice cream cone invented for?

    A. To hold pens
    B. To use in bowling
    C. To hold flowers
    D. To eat by itself

26. Who is the first billionaire player in NBA history?

    A. Michael Jordan
    B. Magic Johnson
    C. Kobe Bryant
    D. Karl Malone

27. What was the top speed of Concorde in miles per hour?

    A. 550 mph
    B. 834 mph
    C. 1000 mph
    D. 1354 mph

28. The kiwi is native to which country?

    A. Australia
    B. Solomon Islands
    C. New Zealand
    D. Fiji

29. With which team has Pau Gasol won two NBA championships?

    A. Chicago Bulls
    B. Los Angeles Lakers
    C. Memphis Grizzlies
    D. San Antonio Spurs

30. Which country has the most Olympic medals?

    A. USA
    B. China
    C. Australia
    D. Spain

31. What is the national dish of Spain?

    A. Queso manchego
    B. Tapas
    C. Paella
    D. Patatas Bravas

32. What are people who love eating ice called?

    A. Iconoclasts
    B. Aquaphages
    C. Pagophagiacs
    D. Dontists

33. The traditional Wimbledon colors are green and what?

   A. Grey
   B. Red Sea
   C. Purple
   D. Orange

34. What was the name of the super concert in 1985?

   A. Woodstock
   B. Live Aid
   C. US Festival
   D. Glastonbury

35. Europe is separated from Africa by which sea?

   A. Mediterranean Sea
   B. Black Sea
   C. Red Sea
   D. Balkan Sea

36. What was Ho Chi Minh city originally called?

   A. Saigon
   B. Laos
   C. Hanoi
   D. Hue

37. What is the official and current name of Big Ben?

    A. Clock Tower
    B. Bell Tower
    C. Elizabeth Tower
    D. Victoria Tower

38. What was the first name of the first human in space?

    A. Vladimir
    B. Tom
    C. Joseph
    D. Yuri

39. Who was the cartoonist behind the Far Side Gallery?

    A. Scott Adams
    B. Robert Crumb
    C. Gary Larson
    D. Walt Disney

40. Nairobi is the capital of which country?

    A. Kenya
    B. Ukraine
    C. Libya
    D. Guatemala

41. Which King of England broke apart from the Catholic Church?

    A. John
    B. Henry VIII
    C. Charles II
    D. George

42. How many elements are in the period table?

    A. 98
    B. 103
    C. 112
    D. 118

43. Which art movement is Salvador Dali associated with?

    A. Abstract
    B. Surrealism
    C. Conceptualism
    D. Expressionism

44. Where might you keep bees?

    A. apiary
    B. aquarium
    C. aviary
    D. vivarium

45. Which among these countries is still led by a monarch?

    A. Saudi Arabia
    B. Egypt
    C. Portugal
    D. France

46. Which country is NOT part of the Mediterranean?

    A. Italy
    B. Greece
    C. Germany
    D. Spain

47. Who invented the radio?

    A. Alexander Graham Bell
    B. Thomas Edison
    C. Philo Taylor Farnsworth
    D. Guglielmo Marconi

48. Which of these elements is not a metal?

    A. mercury
    B. neon
    C. sodium
    D. tungsten

49. Which of these animals lays eggs?

    A. bat
    B. echidna
    C. hedgehog
    D. pangolin

50. What type of business did Annie have that failed in Bridesmaids?

    A. Bakery
    B. Tailor
    C. Cafe
    D. Florist

51. In Roman Myth Mars is the god of what?

    A. Games
    B. love
    C. war
    D. law

52. Which is the oldest continuously inhabited city?

    A. Damascus
    B. Jericho
    C. London
    D. Athens

53. Who said this was their finest hour?

    A. Tony Blair

    B. Winston Churchill

    C. Woodrow Wilson

    D. John Adams

54. What was Veritas the god of?

    A. Beauty

    B. love

    C. peace

    D. truth

55. Which planet has the longest day?

    A. Jupiter

    B. Mercury

    C. Neptune

    D. Venus

56. Cockroaches do what every fifteen minutes?

    A. Pee

    B. Fart

    C. Lay eggs

    D. Twitch

57. The Paris Peace Accords ended which conflict?

    A. WWI
    B. WWII
    C. Vietnam War
    D. Korean War

58. Which is the only Grand Slam tournament that is played on grass?

    A. Wimbledon
    B. French Open
    C. US Open
    D. Australian Open

59. In which city did the Napoleonic wars end?

    A. Ligny
    B. Paris
    C. Waterloo
    D. Wavre

60. What year did the Black death arrive in England?

    A. 1350
    B. 1325
    C. 1300
    D. 1346

61. Which country is closest to the Great Barrier Reef?

    A. USA
    B. Australia
    C. India
    D. Canada

62. What country was formerly called Siam?

    A. Laos
    B. Indonesia
    C. Iran
    D. Thailand

63. Which author's last words were I want nothing but death?

    A. Mark Twain
    B. Jane Austen
    C. Louisa Alcott
    D. Mary Shelley

64. Adobo is a dish that originated from which country?

    A. Thailand
    B. Spain
    C. Portugal
    D. Philippines

65. Where did Rene Descartes spend the last year of his life?

    A. France
    B. Belgium
    C. Sweden
    D. Denmark

66. Which is the world's smallest bird?

    A. hummingbird
    B. verdin
    C. weebill
    D. wren

67. What type of music helps plants grow?

    A. Jazz
    B. New Age
    C. Classical
    D. Pop

68. What is the wine capital of the world?

    A. Adelaide
    B. California
    C. Bordeaux
    D. Paris

69. What is the driest place on the earth?

    A. Death Valley in California
    B. The Dry Valleys in Antartica
    C. The Gobi Desert in China
    D. The Atacama Desert in Chile

70. What is the lowest army rank of a US soldier?

    A. Private
    B. Corporal
    C. Specialist
    D. Sergeant

71. A crepuscular animal becomes active at what time?

    A. Daytime
    B. Nighttime
    C. Dusk
    D. Dawn

72. Which country did bagels originate from?

    A. Germany
    B. USA
    C. Poland
    D. Russia

73. Which horoscope sign has a crab?

    A. Gemini
    B. Pisces
    C. Scorpio
    D. Cancer

74. Who wrote Frankenstein?

    A. Mary Shelley
    B. Percy Shelley
    C. Franklin Stein
    D. Howard Young

75. What is the only Portuguese-speaking country in the Americas?

    A. Brazil
    B. Argentina
    C. Uruguay
    D. Central America

76. Which instrument is associated with Earl Bud Powell?

    A. Bass
    B. Guitar
    C. Flute
    D. Piano

77. Where was the telescope invented?

    A. England

    B. Germany

    C. Italy

    D. Japan

78. Lemons originated from which country?

    A. India

    B. USA

    C. Australia

    D. New Zealand

79. Who wrote Flowers for Algernon?

    A. Herman Hesse

    B. Philip Roth

    C. Daniel Keyes

    D. Ira Levin

80. What was the first name of the first American born saint?

    A. Anne

    B. Martha

    C. Elizabeth

    D. Paul

81. What famous actress once tried to hire a hitman to kill her?

    A. Anne Hathaway
    B. Angelina Jolie
    C. Helen Mirren
    D. Kate Holmes

82. What is an ice hockey puck made from?

    A. Rubber
    B. Plastic
    C. Metal
    D. An alloy

83. According to Greek mythology who was the first woman on earth?

    A. Pandora
    B. Hera
    C. Persephone
    D. Medea

84. Where was the world's smallest fish discovered?

    A. Indonesia
    B. Brazil
    C. Australia
    D. Turkey

85. Which country is the least populated?

    A. Vatican City
    B. Palau
    C. Monaco
    D. San Marino

86. Shintoism originated from which country?

    A. India
    B. South Korea
    C. Japan
    D. Thailand

87. What's the best known artificial international language?

    A. Esperanto
    B. Esperanzo
    C. Elfin
    D. Elven

88. Name the only New York Yankee to hit four home runs in one game?

    A. Ty Cobb
    B. Joe DiMaggio
    C. Micky Mantle
    D. Lou Gehrig

89. Which country has the lowest crime rate?

    A. Canada

    B. Iceland

    C. USA

    D. Bolivia

90. Which colour has the highest frequency in the visible spectrum?

    A. blue

    B. indigo

    C. red

    D. violet

91. What year did the Spanish civil war occur?

    A. 1920

    B. 1930

    C. 1936

    D. 1940

92. Which is the brightest planet as seen from earth?

    A. Jupiter

    B. Mars

    C. Saturn

    D. Venus

93. The world's largest theme park is located in which country?

    A. USA
    B. Japan
    C. France
    D. Brazil

94. How many hearts does an octopus have?

    A. 1
    B. 3
    C. 4
    D. 8

95. Where did rap superstar Eminem grow up?

    A. Detroit
    B. Chicago
    C. St. Louis
    D. Los Angeles

96. What year did Queen Victoria become Queen?

    A. 1845
    B. 1829
    C. 1835
    D. 1837

97. What is the softest mineral in the world?

A. Diamond
B. Calcite
C. Talc
D. Apatite

98. Which creatures produce gossamer?

A. Silkworms
B. A spider
C. Moths
D. Caterpillars

99. A riel is the currency of which country?

A. Kyrgyzstan
B. Mongolia
C. Cambodia
D. Myanmar

100. The southern tip of South America has what name?

A. Cape Horn
B. Cape Town
C. Ushuaia
D. Buenos Aires

101. Which type of fruit juice did Dole sell first?

   A. Cranberry
   B. Pineapple
   C. Grape
   D. Tomato

102. Which English city has more miles of canals than Venice?

   A. Birmingham
   B. Colchester
   C. Manchester
   D. Coventry

103. Which is the heaviest living bird species?

   A. emu
   B. penguin
   C. ostrich
   D. rhea

104. Which U.S. President served 3 terms?

   A. Roosevelt
   B. Washington
   C. Carter
   D. Adams

105. In what year was the first ever Wimbledon Championship held?

    A. 1877
    B. 1881
    C. 1911
    D. 1900

106. How many signs are there in the Zodiac?

    A. 10
    B. 12
    C. 8
    D. 14

107. Mt. Everest is located in which country?

    A. Nepal
    B. USA
    C. Canada
    D. India

108. Who was Catherine the Great's husband?

    A. Ivan I
    B. Peter III
    C. Paul I
    D. Peter II

109. Where was the world's first University located?

    A. Alexandria
    B. Constantinople
    C. Rome
    D. Athens

110. What did Harriet Tubman suffer from as a child?

    A. Head injury
    B. smallpox
    C. influenza
    D. leg injury

111. What was Babe Ruth's first name?

    A. George
    B. Gregory
    C. Gerald
    D. Gary

112. How many hearts does an octopus have?

    A. Four
    B. Three
    C. Two
    D. Six

113. What was the name of the first satellite launched into space?

   A. Atlas
   B. Apollo I
   C. Mir
   D. Sputnik I

114. How many years did Charles Darwin wait to publish his findings?

   A. 1
   B. 5
   C. 10
   D. 20

115. What was branch of science was Ernest Rutherford famous for?

   A. botany
   B. meteorology
   C. paleontology
   D. radioactivity

116. What is the name of the Earth's largest ocean?

   A. Pacific Ocean
   B. Atlantic Ocean
   C. Artic Ocean
   D. Indian Ocean

117. What is the most abundant element in the known universe?

    A. carbon
    B. hydrogen
    C. iron
    D. nitrogen

118. By which nickname was Evander Holyfield popularly known?

    A. The Mongoose
    B. The Real Deal
    C. Easton Assassin
    D. Evander Holyfield

119. Water has a pH level of around?

    A. 7
    B. 9
    C. 12
    D. 5

120. What year did Canada become a country?

    A. 1867
    B. 1870
    C. 1890
    D. 1857

121. Who voices Morty in the series Rick and Morty?

    A. Robert Redford
    B. Gray Jackson
    C. Justin Rolland
    D. Toni Scarroli

122. Humans have 7 neck vertebrae. How many do giraffes have?

    A. 4
    B. 7
    C. 10
    D. 14

123. What is the Higgs boson?

    A. element
    B. molecule
    C. subatomic particle
    D. theory of gravity

124. What is the largest continent by population?

    A. Europe
    B. Asia
    C. Africa
    D. North America

125. Where would you find the smallest bones in the human body?

    A. ear
    B. finger
    C. spine
    D. toe

126. Where is the Easter Island located?

    A. Chile
    B. China
    C. Morocco
    D. Singapore

127. The world's biggest pyramid is located in which country?

    A. China
    B. Egypt
    C. Mexico
    D. Argentina

128. It is illegal to do what in the French vineyards?

    A. Have a picnic
    B. Curse
    C. Die
    D. Land a flying saucer

129. A puffball is a type of what?

   A. fish
   B. frog
   C. fungi
   D. parrot

130. Who sang about being an eggman and a walrus?

   A. The Beatles
   B. The Eagles
   C. The Drivers
   D. The Lovers

131. In which country is the Troi-Rivieres bridge?

   A. France
   B. Canada
   C. Vietnam
   D. Algeria

132. Which Tasmanian marsupial is known for its temper?

   A. Possums
   B. Kangaroos
   C. Tasmanian Devil
   D. Koalas

133. Bicycles were first used in which country?

   A. Germany
   B. Thailand
   C. France
   D. Denmark

134. What is the legislature of the Netherlands called?

   A. The Collective Meeting
   B. The States General
   C. The General Legislature
   D. The People's Congress

135. Which country did Winston Churchill lead during WWII?

   A. U.K
   B. Canada
   C. Spain
   D. France

136. What is the main component of Saturn's rings?

   A. dust
   B. gas
   C. ice
   D. rock

137. Where is the Large Hadron Collider?

    A. Austria
    B. Sweden
    C. Switzerland
    D. United Kingdom

138. In 1917 Finland declared its independence from which country?

    A. Sweden
    B. Norway
    C. Denmark
    D. Russia

139. Which of these items was not invented by Leonardo da Vinci

    A. bicycle
    B. diving suit
    C. helicopter
    D. parachute

140. In which city did Anne Frank hide from the Nazis?

    A. Berlin
    B. Paris
    C. Warsaw
    D. Amsterdam

141. How many time zones does Russia span?

    A. 6

    B. 7

    C. 11

    D. 15

142. Platypus are endemic to which county?

    A. Australia

    B. Ecuador

    C. Brazil

    D. USA

143. By which nickname were Stephen Curry and Klay Thompson known as?

    A. Bruise Brothers

    B. Splash Brothers

    C. Twin Towers

    D. Death Lineup

144. Around how many countries have a royal family?

    A. 12

    B. 25

    C. 43

    D. 5

145. What was France originally called?

   A. Gaul
   B. Lutetia
   C. Lyon
   D. Merea

146. How would you write the number 5 in binary code?

   A. 1
   B. 11
   C. 101
   D. 111

147. In which of Britney's video does she appear as a stewardess?

   A. ... Baby One More Time
   B. Womanizer
   C. Toxic
   D. Pretty Girls

148. The longest NBA game occurred between:

   A. Chicago Bulls and Miami Heat
   B. Detroit Pistons and Denver Nuggets
   C. Boston Celtics and Minneapolis Lakers
   D. Indianapolis Olympians and Rochester Royals

149. What does the word Matrix mean in the Bible?

    A. Womb
    B. Burial place
    C. Heaven
    D. Prophet

150. How long was the Vietnam war?

    A. 14 years
    B. 15 years
    C. 19 years
    D. 18 years

151. Which Battle was fought mostly in the air?

    A. Britain
    B. Stalingrad
    C. Somme
    D. Vimy Ridge

152. Who was the only US President to resign?

    A. Gerald Ford
    B. Richard Nixon
    C. William McKinley
    D. William Taft

153. What is the most abundant element in the universe?

    A. Hydrogen
    B. Oxygen
    C. Carbon
    D. Neon

154. Which human has the most bones?

    A. adult female
    B. adult male
    C. baby
    D. teenager

155. What is the name of the cells in the eye that detect color?

    A. cones
    B. iris
    C. retina
    D. rods

156. How many French Open titles has Rafael Nadal won?

    A. 10
    B. 8
    C. 12
    D. 13

157. Which country is considered as land locked?

    A. Greenland
    B. Kazakhstan
    C. Portugal
    D. Pakistan

158. Which Philosopher tutored Alexander the Great?

    A. Plato
    B. Isocrates
    C. Ptolemy
    D. Aristotle

159. What year did Harriet Tubman escape slavery?

    A. 1850
    B. 1845
    C. 1849
    D. 1840

160. In what city did Princess Diana suffer her fatal car crash?

    A. London
    B. Madrid
    C. Rome
    D. Paris

161. Who was the first explorer to reach the North Pole?

    A. Chistopher Columbus
    B. James Cook
    C. Robert Peary
    D. James Clark Ross

162. How much DNA do humans share with bananas?

    A. 0%
    B. 5%
    C. 50%
    D. 90%

163. How many time zones does the United States have?

    A. 12
    B. 9
    C. 5
    D. 14

164. What is the tiny piece at the end of a shoelace called?

    A. Aglet
    B. Edge
    C. Clasp
    D. Catch

165. What is the longest mountain range in the world?

    A. Alaska Range
    B. Andes
    C. Himalayas
    D. Tian Shan

166. Which ocean is the Bermuda Triangle located?

    A. North Atlantic
    B. Pacific
    C. Indian
    D. Arctic

167. Which city was the ASPCA founded in?

    A. New York City
    B. Pittsburgh
    C. Denver
    D. Chicago

168. Which civilization invented the wheel?

    A. Egypt
    B. China
    C. Rome
    D. Mesopotamia

169. Dendrophobia is the fear of what?

    A. Flowers
    B. Trees
    C. The Night Sky
    D. Wind

170. The Sudanese Republic is now which country?

    A. Mali
    B. Guinea
    C. Ghana
    D. South Sudan

171. Monica Seles was stabbed by an obsessed fan of this player:

    A. Jennifer Capriati
    B. Lindsay Davenport
    C. Chris Evert
    D. Steffi Graf

172. Which among these cities is NOT a capital?

    A. Pyongyang
    B. Amsterdam
    C. Manila
    D. Toronto

173. Other than a General what was Stonewall Jackson other career?

    A. Carpentry
    B. lawyer
    C. teacher
    D. merchant

174. What is the state capital of New York?

    A. New York City
    B. Albany
    C. Rochester
    D. Utica

175. Who is this boxer who lost 31of his 32 bouts via knockout?

    A. Harold Brazier
    B. Eric Crumble
    C. Antwun Echols
    D. Bennie Briscoe

176. Which fruit floats because 25% of its volume is air?

    A. Pomegranate
    B. Honeydew
    C. Strawberry
    D. Apple

177. Who is the only non-American to win all four majors in a career?

A. Bernhard Langer
B. Vijay Singh
C. Gary Player
D. Sergio Garcia

178. How old was Mike Tyson when he became the heavyweight champion?

A. 20
B. 22
C. 24
D. 26

179. The Treaty of Ghent was the peace treaty that ended which war?

A. The Seven Years War
B. World War I
C. The Russian Revolution
D. The War of 1812

180. What is the capital city of Canada's Yukon territory?

A. Edmonton
B. Whitehorse
C. Banff
D. Moose Jaw

181. How many provinces does China have?

    A. 23

    B. 13

    C. 10

    D. 34

182. Which gas makes up 91% of the sun?

    A. helium

    B. hydrogen

    C. nitrogen

    D. oxygen

183. In June in Wyoming it is illegal to take a picture of what?

    A. An elk

    B. A bison

    C. A geyser

    D. A rabbit

184. What is the capital of Germany?

    A. Cologne

    B. Munich

    C. Berlin

    D. Hamburg

185. Which continent is in all four hemispheres?

   A. Africa
   B. Asia
   C. Antarctica
   D. Europe

186. What kind of animal is a firefly?

   A. Fly
   B. Beetle
   C. Moth
   D. Bee

187. The video game Happy Feet features what animals?

   A. Penguins
   B. Giraffes
   C. Hippos
   D. Cats

188. Which animal was the main cause of the Bubonic Plague?

   A. Rats
   B. Rabbits
   C. Cats
   D. Birds

189. A joule is a measurement of what?

   A. energy
   B. force
   C. mass
   D. speed

190. What type of tree grows from an acorn?

   A. elm
   B. fir
   C. maple
   D. oak

191. Botany is the scientific study of what?

   A. Flowers
   B. Plants
   C. Biomes
   D. Bugs

192. What is the longest river in Australia?

   A. The Murray River
   B. The Darling River
   C. Lachlan River
   D. Cooper Creek

193. How many Theses did Martine Luther write?

   A. 99
   B. 100
   C. 90
   D. 95

194. What is the chemical symbol for silver?

   A. Ag
   B. Au
   C. Si
   D. Sr

195. Dmitri Mendeleev worked in which field of science?

   A. astronomy
   B. botany
   C. chemistry
   D. quantum physics

196. Which of these is not a type of quark?

   A. charm
   B. down
   C. round
   D. up

197. Where did the first hot air Balloon ride take place?

    A. Berlin
    B. Paris
    C. London
    D. Madrid

198. Charles Darwin is famous for the theory of what?

    A. continental drift
    B. evolution
    C. relativity
    D. the big bang

199. What did Russia abolish in 1861?

    A. Serfdom
    B. child labor
    C. capital punishment
    D. child marriage

200. What did Ada Lovelace Study?

    A. Mathematics
    B. history
    C. biology
    D. literature

SECTION 1
ANSWERS

1. Which is the largest living animal on earth?

   Blue whale

2. When a people are frightened their ears produce more of what?

   Earwax

3. Which type of infection could be treated with antibiotics?

   Bacterial infection

4. New York City comprises how many boroughs?

   5

5. The aardvark is native to which continent?

   Africa

6. Which Dutch artist painted Girl with a Pearl Earring?

   Vermeer

7. What happened in the Soviet Union from 1933-1934?

   Famine

8. What was Toyota's first popular hybrid car called?

   Prius

9. What of these animals is not an amphibian?

Eel

10. Tim Berners-Lee is credited with the invention of what?

World Wide Web

11. What is a baby goat called?

A kid

12. Which country is known as the Land of White Elephant?

Thailand

13. Which US state is also called the Aloha State?

Hawaii

14. What percentage of all species on earth are insects?

80%

15. Where do kiwi fruits originally come from?

China

16. How did Anne Frank receive her diary?

birthday gift

17. What is the driest continent?

    Antartica

18. How old was Marie Antoinette when she married?

    14

19. What is the capital of Australia?

    Canberra

20. How many countries have names that end in -stan?

    7

21. Which country is the largest rice producer?

    China

22. What was the first fruit that was eaten on the moon?

    Peach

23. In which European city would you find Orly airport?

    Paris

24. Who claimed he could drive away the devil with a fart?

    Martin Luther

25. What was the ice cream cone invented for?

   To hold flowers

26. Who is the first billionaire player in NBA history?

   Michael Jordan

27. What was the top speed of Concorde in miles per hour?

   1354 mph

28. The kiwi is native to which country?

   New Zealand

29. With which team has Pau Gasol won two NBA championships?

   Los Angeles Lakers

30. Which country has the most Olympic medals?

   USA

31. What is the national dish of Spain?

   Paella

32. What are people who love eating ice called?

   Pagophagiacs

33. The traditional Wimbledon colors are green and what?

    Purple

34. What was the name of the super concert in 1985?

    Live Aid

35. Europe is separated from Africa by which sea?

    Mediterranean Sea

36. What was Ho Chi Minh city originally called?

    Saigon

37. What is the official and current name of Big Ben?

    Elizabeth Tower

38. What was the first name of the first human in space?

    Yuri

39. Who was the cartoonist behind the Far Side Gallery?

    Gary Larson

40. Nairobi is the capital of which country?

    Kenya

41. Which King of England broke apart from the Catholic Church?

   Henry VIII

42. How many elements are in the period table?

   118

43. Which art movement is Salvador Dali associated with?

   Surrealism

44. Where might you keep bees?

   Apiary

45. Which among these countries is still led by a monarch?

   Saudi Arabia

46. Which country is NOT part of the Mediterranean?

   Germany

47. Who invented the radio?

   Guglielmo Marconi

48. Which of these elements is not a metal?

   Neon

49. Which of these animals lays eggs?

    Echidna

50. What type of business did Annie have that failed in Bridesmaids?

    Bakery

51. In Roman Myth Mars is the god of what?

    war

52. Which is the oldest continuously inhabited city?

    Damascus

53. Who said this was their finest hour?

    Winston Churchill

54. What was Veritas the god of?

    truth

55. Which planet has the longest day?

    Venus

56. Cockroaches do what every fifteen minutes?

    Fart

57. The Paris Peace Accords ended which conflict?

Vietnam War

58. Which is the only Grand Slam tournament that is played on grass?

Wimbledon

59. In which city did the Napoleonic wars end?

Waterloo

60. What year did the Black death arrive in England?

1346

61. Which country is closest to the Great Barrier Reef?

Australia

62. What country was formerly called Siam?

Thailand

63. Which author's last words were I want nothing but death?

Jane Austen

64. Adobo is a dish that originated from which country?

Philippines

65. Where did Rene Descartes spend the last year of his life?

   Sweden

66. Which is the world's smallest bird?

   Hummingbird

67. What type of music helps plants grow?

   Classical

68. What is the wine capital of the world?

   Bordeaux

69. What is the driest place on the earth?

   The Dry Valleys in Antartica

70. What is the lowest army rank of a US soldier?

   Private

71. A crepuscular animal becomes active at what time?

   Dusk

72. Which country did bagels originate from?

   Poland

73. Which horoscope sign has a crab?

Cancer

74. Who wrote Frankenstein?

Mary Shelley

75. What is the only Portuguese-speaking country in the Americas?

Brazil

76. Which instrument is associated with Earl Bud Powell?

Piano

77. Where was the telescope invented?

England

78. Lemons originated from which country?

India

79. Who wrote Flowers for Algernon?

Daniel Keyes

80. What was the first name of the first American born saint?

Elizabeth

81. What famous actress once tried to hire a hitman to kill her?

Angelina Jolie

82. What is an ice hockey puck made from?

Rubber

83. According to Greek mythology who was the first woman on earth?

Pandora

84. Where was the world's smallest fish discovered?

Indonesia

85. Which country is the least populated?

Vatican City

86. Shintoism originated from which country?

Japan

87. What's the best known artificial international language?

Esperanto

88. Name the only New York Yankee to hit four home runs in one game?

Lou Gehrig

89. Which country has the lowest crime rate?

   Iceland

90. Which colour has the highest frequency in the visible spectrum?

   Violet

91. What year did the Spanish civil war occur?

   1936

92. Which is the brightest planet as seen from earth?

   Venus

93. The world's largest theme park is located in which country?

   USA

94. How many hearts does an octopus have?

   3

95. Where did rap superstar Eminem grow up?

   Detroit

96. What year did Queen Victoria become Queen?

   1837

97. What is the softest mineral in the world?

Talc

98. Which creatures produce gossamer?

A spider

99. A riel is the currency of which country?

Cambodia

100. The southern tip of South America has what name?

Cape Horn

101. Which type of fruit juice did Dole sell first?

Pineapple

102. Which English city has more miles of canals than Venice?

Birmingham

103. Which is the heaviest living bird species?

Ostrich

104. Which U.S. President served 3 terms?

Roosevelt

105. In what year was the first ever Wimbledon Championship held?

1877

106. How many signs are there in the Zodiac?

12

107. Mt. Everest is located in which country?

Nepal

108. Who was Catherine the Great's husband?

Peter III

109. Where was the world's first University located?

Constantinople

110. What did Harriet Tubman suffer from as a child?

head injury

111. What was Babe Ruth's first name?

George

112. How many hearts does an octopus have?

Three

113. What was the name of the first satellite launched into space?

Sputnik I

114. How many years did Charles Darwin wait to publish his findings?

20

115. What was branch of science was Ernest Rutherford famous for?

Radioactivity

116. What is the name of the Earth's largest ocean?

The Pacific Ocean

117. What is the most abundant element in the known universe?

Hydrogen

118. By which nickname was Evander Holyfield popularly known?

The Real Deal

119. Water has a pH level of around?

7

120. What year did Canada become a country?

1867

121. Who voices Morty in the series Rick and Morty?

Justin Rolland

122. Humans have 7 neck vertebrae. How many do giraffes have?

7

123. What is the Higgs boson?

Subatomic particle

124. What is the largest continent by population?

Asia

125. Where would you find the smallest bones in the human body?

Ear

126. Where is the Easter Island located?

Chile

127. The world's biggest pyramid is located in which country?

Mexico

128. It is illegal to do what in the French vineyards?

Land a flying saucer

129. A puffball is a type of what?

Fungi

130. Who sang about being an eggman and a walrus?

The Beatles

131. In which country is the Troi-Rivieres bridge?

Canada

132. Which Tasmanian marsupial is known for its temper?

Tasmanian Devil

133. Bicycles were first used in which country?

Germany

134. What is the legislature of the Netherlands called?

The States General

135. Which country did Winston Churchill lead during WWII?

U.K.

136. What is the main component of Saturn's rings?

Ice

137. Where is the Large Hadron Collider?

Switzerland

138. In 1917 Finland declared its independence from which country?

Russia

139. Which of these items was not invented by Leonardo da Vinci

Bicycle

140. In which city did Anne Frank hide from the Nazis?

Amsterdam

141. How many time zones does Russia span?

11

142. Platypus are endemic to which county?

Australia

143. By which nickname were Stephen Curry and Klay Thompson known as?

Splash Brothers

144. Around how many countries have a royal family?

43

145. What was France originally called?

Gaul

146. How would you write the number 5 in binary code?

101

147. In which of Britney's video does she appear as a stewardess?

Toxic

148. The longest NBA game occurred between:

Indianapolis Olympians and Rochester Royals

149. What does the word Matrix mean in the Bible?

Womb

150. How long was the Vietnam war?

19 years

151. Which Battle was fought mostly in the air?

Britain

152. Who was the only US President to resign?

Richard Nixon

153. What is the most abundant element in the universe?

Hydrogen

154. Which human has the most bones?

Baby

155. What is the name of the cells in the eye that detect color?

Cones

156. How many French Open titles has Rafael Nadal won?

12

157. Which country is considered as land locked?

Kazakhstan

158. Which Philosopher tutored Alexander the Great?

Aristotle

159. What year did Harriet Tubman escape slavery?

1849

160. In what city did Princess Diana suffer her fatal car crash?

Paris

161. Who was the first explorer to reach the North Pole?

Robert Peary

162. How much DNA do humans share with bananas?

50%

163. How many time zones does the United States have?

9

164. What is the tiny piece at the end of a shoelace called?

Aglet

165. What is the longest mountain range in the world?

Andes

166. Which ocean is the Bermuda Triangle located?

North Atlantic

167. Which city was the ASPCA founded in?

New York City

168. Which civilization invented the wheel?

Mesopotamia

169. Dendrophobia is the fear of what?

Trees

170. The Sudanese Republic is now which country?

Mali

171. Monica Seles was stabbed by an obsessed fan of this player:

Steffi Graf

172. Which among these cities is NOT a capital?

Toronto

173. Other than a General what was Stonewall Jackson other career?

teacher

174. What is the state capital of New York?

Albany

175. Who is this boxer who lost 31of his 32 bouts via knockout?

Eric Crumble

176. Which fruit floats because 25% of its volume is air?

Apple

177. Who is the only non-American to win all four majors in a career?

Gary Player

178. How old was Mike Tyson when he became the heavyweight champion?

20

179. The Treaty of Ghent was the peace treaty that ended which war?

The War of 1812

180. What is the capital city of Canada's Yukon territory?

Whitehorse

181. How many provinces does China have?

23

182. Which gas makes up 91% of the sun?

Hydrogen

183. In June in Wyoming it is illegal to take a picture of what?

A rabbit

184. What is the capital of Germany?

Berlin

185. Which continent is in all four hemispheres?

Africa

186. What kind of animal is a firefly?

Beetle

187. The video game Happy Feet features what animals?

Penguins

188. Which animal was the main cause of the Bubonic Plague?

Rats

189. A joule is a measurement of what?

Energy

190. What type of tree grows from an acorn?

Oak

191. Botany is the scientific study of what?

Plants

192. What is the longest river in Australia?

The Murray River

193. How many Theses did Martine Luther write?

95

194. What is the chemical symbol for silver?

Ag

195. Dmitri Mendeleev worked in which field of science?

Chemistry

196. Which of these is not a type of quark?

Round

197. Where did the first hot air Balloon ride take place?

Paris

198. Charles Darwin is famous for the theory of what?

Evolution

199. What did Russia abolish in 1861?

serfdom

200. What did Ada Lovelace Study?

mathematics

SECTION 2

1. What is the official and current name of Big Ben?

    A. Clock Tower
    B. Bell Tower
    C. Elizabeth Tower
    D. Victoria Tower

2. What did Alexander Fleming famously discover?

    A. DNA
    B. gravity
    C. penicillin
    D. vaccinations

3. Martin Luther sparked which event?

    A. French Revolution
    B. Crimean War
    C. Protestant Reformation
    D. WWI

4. How many countries are in Asia?

    A. 52
    B. 70
    C. 48
    D. 65

5. Where is Angkor Wat located?

    A. Cambodia
    B. Laos
    C. Thailand
    D. Indonesia

6. What's the most populous city in the United States?

    A. New York City
    B. Los Angeles
    C. Chicago
    D. Houston

7. Who was the longest-serving U.K. Prime Minister?

    A. Robert Walpole
    B. William Pitt
    C. Tony Blair
    D. David Cameron

8. Which dynasty build most of the Great Wall of China?

    A. Shang
    B. Zhou
    C. Ming
    D. Yuan

9. What is the function of a xylem in a plant?

    A. nutrient storage

    B. reproduction

    C. photosynthesis

    D. transport of water

10. In 1979 the USSR invaded which country?

    A. China

    B. Iran

    C. Afghanistan

    D. Ukraine

11. What were the earliest forms of contraceptive made from?

    A. Papyrus Leaves

    B. Beetles

    C. Wheat

    D. Crocodile Dung

12. What is the fastest growing plant on earth?

    A. algae

    B. bamboo

    C. eucalyptus

    D. sequoia

13. Port-au-Prince is the capital of which country?

A. Dominican Republic
B. Haiti
C. Suriname
D. Grenada

14. A cross appears in the flags of these countries except?

A. Tonga
B. Georgia
C. Switzerland
D. Spain

15. Which is the largest living lizard on earth?

A. crocodile
B. goanna
C. iguana
D. Komodo dragon

16. Which below sea level mountain is taller than Mt. Everest?

A. Mauna Kea
B. Mount Vema
C. Maud Seamount
D. Belgica Guyot

17. Yao Ming played for this NBA team:

    A. Houston Rockets
    B. Golden State Warriors
    C. New Orleans Pelicans
    D. Atlanta Hawks

18. What was discovered in the Yukon in 1896?

    A. Dinosaur fossils
    B. gold
    C. oil
    D. ancient tribe

19. A manatee is also known as what?

    A. sea cow
    B. sea elephant
    C. sea horse
    D. sea lion

20. Which was the first living creature to be sent to space?

    A. dog
    B. fruit fly
    C. gerbil
    D. mouse

21. What is the main ingredient in falafel?

    A. Lentils
    B. Rice
    C. Chickpea
    D. Bulghar

22. Who said this was their finest hour?

    A. Tony Blair
    B. Winston Churchill
    C. Woodrow Wilson
    D. John Adams

23. What is secreted from the lacrimal gland?

    A. adrenaline
    B. saliva
    C. sweat
    D. tears

24. What is the name of the book written by Bobby Fischer?

    A. My System
    B. The Inner Game
    C. Endgame Manual
    D. My 60 Memorable Games

25. Dutch people live in which country?

   A. Georgia
   B. Netherlands
   C. Belgium
   D. Denmark

26. Which among these states is NOT in the East Coast?

   A. Maine
   B. Oregon
   C. New York
   D. Florida

27. What is the largest lizard?

   A. Gila
   B. Water dragon
   C. Komodo dragon
   D. Alligator

28. Mt. Everest is located in which country?

   A. Nepal
   B. USA
   C. Canada
   D. India

29. What type of music helps plants grow?

    A. Jazz
    B. New Age
    C. Classical
    D. Pop

30. Which element has the symbol Pb?

    A. gold
    B. lead
    C. potassium
    D. phosphorus

31. Osteoporosis is a disease affecting which part of the body?

    A. blood
    B. bones
    C. brain
    D. skin

32. How long was the Vietnam war?

    A. 14 years
    B. 15 years
    C. 19 years
    D. 18 years

33. Which King of England broke apart from the Catholic Church?

   A. John
   B. Henry VIII
   C. Charles II
   D. George

34. What is the fungi Hydnellum peckii also known as?

   A. Blood cap
   B. Black mold
   C. The golden crown fungus
   D. The bleeding tooth fungus

35. What is the capital of Qatar?

   A. Dukhan
   B. Doha
   C. Abu Dhabi
   D. Dubai

36. Where was the first tank produced?

   A. England
   B. France
   C. Germany
   D. the U.S.

37. Which of the following pH values indicates an acidic solution?

    A. pH1
    B. pH7
    C. pH10
    D. pH14

38. The Petronas Towers is located in what country?

    A. Singapore
    B. Indonesia
    C. Thailand
    D. Malaysia

39. Mount Kilimanjaro is located in which country?

    A. Tanzania
    B. India
    C. USA
    D. Poland

40. The Mayans worshiped which animal as gods?

    A. Horses
    B. cats
    C. rabbits
    D. turkeys

41. Where in your body is your axilla?

    A. ankle

    B. armpit

    C. ear

    D. knee

42. When a people are frightened their ears produce more of what?

    A. Earwax

    B. Sweat

    C. Ringing sounds

    D. White blood cells

43. Which war did George Orwell fight in?

    A. WWI

    B. WWII

    C. the Spanish Civil war

    D. the Russian Civil War

44. What did the first vending machine dispense?

    A. Holy Water

    B. Cigarettes

    C. Candy

    D. Soda

45. Distance is equal to speed multiplied by what?

  A. acceleration
  B. length
  C. time
  D. velocity

46. What is the only bird known to fly backwards?

  A. Sparrow
  B. Hummingbird
  C. Cape Teal
  D. White Headed Petril

47. What was Marilyn Monroe's natural hair color?

  A. Brunette
  B. Blonde
  C. Black
  D. Red

48. Where did rap superstar Eminem grow up?

  A. Detroit
  B. Chicago
  C. St. Louis
  D. Los Angeles

49. Where is the Stone Henge located?

    A. England
    B. Netherlands
    C. Pakistan
    D. Brazil

50. Caesar salad originated from which country?

    A. Italy
    B. Mexico
    C. France
    D. Italy

51. What is dendrochronology?

    A. climate science
    B. study of skin
    C. study of teeth
    D. tree-ring dating

52. How long can a cockroach survive without its head?

    A. 2 minutes
    B. 24 hours
    C. 2 days
    D. 1 week

53. Which of the following numbers is a prime number?

    A. 6
    B. 9
    C. 13
    D. 15

54. Where do natural pearls comes from?

    A. ice
    B. rock ore
    C. oysters
    D. whales

55. A pangolin is a type of what?

    A. amphibian
    B. fish
    C. mammal
    D. reptile

56. What is the loudest animal on Earth?

    A. Elephant
    B. Lion
    C. The Blue Whale
    D. The sperm whale

57. Complete the title of a 1979 number one by Blondie Heart of...

    A. Glass
    B. Gold
    C. Platinum
    D. Steel

58. What color does gold leaf appear if you hold it up to the light?

    A. Blue
    B. Green
    C. Violet
    D. Amber

59. How was the Library of Alexandria destroyed?

    A. Tornado
    B. volcano
    C. fire
    D. hurricane

60. Which US state has the smallest population?

    A. New Mexico
    B. Louisiana
    C. Maine
    D. Wyoming

61. Cirque du Soleil started in what country?

    A. Canada

    B. France

    C. Italy

    D. Mexico

62. Around how many countries have a royal family?

    A. 12

    B. 25

    C. 43

    D. 5

63. Power outages in the US are mostly caused by what?

    A. Lightning

    B. Earthquakes

    C. Squirrels

    D. Birds

64. What particle in an atom has a positive charge?

    A. Neutron

    B. Electron

    C. Proton

    D. Quark

65. Who is the youngest winner in any Grand Slam tournament?

    A. Boris Becker
    B. Martina Hingis
    C. Monica Seles
    D. Jennifer Capriati

66. If a male donkey is a jack what is the female called?

    A. Jackie
    B. Regina
    C. Jane
    D. Jenny

67. What year did Harriet Tubman escape slavery?

    A. 1850
    B. 1845
    C. 1849
    D. 1840

68. Nepal is located on which continent?

    A. Asia
    B. Africa
    C. Oceania
    D. South America

69. What is the capital of Germany?

   A. Cologne
   B. Munich
   C. Berlin
   D. Hamburg

70. What is the only Portuguese-speaking country in the Americas?

   A. Brazil
   B. Argentina
   C. Uruguay
   D. Central America

71. Which of these is not a type of wild cat?

   A. dingo
   B. lynx
   C. ocelot
   D. serval

72. Which country owns the Galapagos Islands?

   A. Spain
   B. Ecuador
   C. Papua New Guinea
   D. Portugal

73. Which country is predominantly Buddhist?

    A. Thailand
    B. Slovakia
    C. South Korea
    D. Botswana

74. Susan B. Antony was the first woman to be honored in this way?

    A. Currency
    B. medal of honor
    C. building
    D. law

75. Who established the 365-day calendar?

    A. Augustus
    B. Julius Caesar
    C. Trajan
    D. Henry VI

76. The video game Happy Feet features what animals?

    A. Penguins
    B. Giraffes
    C. Hippos
    D. Cats

77. What language has the most words?

    A. French
    B. English
    C. Chinese
    D. Hindi

78. What is the capital city of Canada's Yukon territory?

    A. Edmonton
    B. Whitehorse
    C. Banff
    D. Moose Jaw

79. What is the name of the Earth's largest ocean?

    A. Pacific Ocean
    B. Atlantic Ocean
    C. Artic Ocean
    D. Indian Ocean

80. Galileo was the citizen of which country?

    A. France
    B. Portugal
    C. Italy
    D. Germany

81. Florence Nightingale aided the sick and wounded during what war?

    A. The Boer Wars
    B. The War of 1812
    C. The Crimean War
    D. The Revolutionary War

82. Where is the Machu Picchu located?

    A. Nepal
    B. Brazil
    C. Peru
    D. Myanmar

83. What is the modern name of Saigon?

    A. Dalat
    B. Ha Long
    C. Ho Chi Minh
    D. Hanoi

84. What is the softest mineral in the world?

    A. Diamond
    B. Calcite
    C. Talc
    D. Apatite

85. Humphrey Bogart won his only Oscar for what motion picture?

    A. The African Queen
    B. Casablanca
    C. Caine Mutiny
    D. The Maltese Falcon

86. Which among these records does Magic Johnson hold?

    A. Oldest player to score 30+ points in a game
    B. Oldest player to score 50+ points in a game
    C. Oldest player to score 40+ points in a game
    D. Youngest to score 50+ points in a game

87. How did Anne Frank receive her diary?

    A. Birthday gift
    B. found it
    C. stole it
    D. bought it herself

88. Where would you find cellulose?

    A. blood cells
    B. plant tissue
    C. rocks
    D. space

89. What is the real first name of Marilyn Monroe?

    A. Norma Jeane
    B. Grace Reed
    C. Daisy Wilder
    D. Regina Mack

90. In which country is divorce illegal?

    A. Philippines
    B. Iran
    C. Somalia
    D. Dominican Republic

91. What did Spain introduce to Ireland in the late 1500s?

    A. Corn
    B. Potatoes
    C. Tomatoes
    D. Beans

92. Which country had a personal union with Denmark?

    A. Norway
    B. Finland
    C. Iceland
    D. Italy

93. Which of these animals lays eggs?

    A. bat
    B. echidna
    C. hedgehog
    D. pangolin

94. In Roman Myth Mars is the god of what?

    A. Games
    B. love
    C. war
    D. law

95. Which is the biggest moon in the solar system?

    A. Ganymede (Jupiter)
    B. Io (Jupiter)
    C. Moon (Earth)
    D. Titan (Saturn)

96. Who lives in a trash can on Sesame Street?

    A. Oscar
    B. Cookie
    C. Elmo
    D. Daffy

97. Which U.S. President was the first to ride in a Helicopter?

    A. Eisenhower
    B. Kennedy
    C. Roosevelt
    D. Truman

98. Where did Leonardo da Vinci spend his final years of life?

    A. England
    B. France
    C. Spain
    D. Italy

99. Hinduism originated from which country?

    A. Pakistan
    B. India
    C. Bangladesh
    D. Afghanistan

100. Who composed the music for Sonic the Hedgehog 3?

    A. Michael Jackson
    B. Billy Joel
    C. Bruce Springsteen
    D. John McCartney

101. Ferrari is from from which country?

   A. Germany
   B. Austria
   C. Spain
   D. Italy

102. Who gifted the Statue of Liberty to the U.S.?

   A. England
   B. Canada
   C. France
   D. Italy

103. NBA basketball legend Kobe Bryant died in:

   A. A plane crash
   B. A helicopter crash
   C. The Covid pandemic
   D. A car crash

104. Marilyn Monroe was married to which famous sportsman?

   A. Yogi Berra
   B. Justin Verlander
   C. Ralph Kiner
   D. Joe DiMaggio

105. Who was the captain of the Titanic?

    A. Robert Fields
    B. J. Bruce Ismay
    C. Alexander Carlisle
    D. Edward Smith

106. Abbey Road is located in which city?

    A. Leeds
    B. Nottingham
    C. London
    D. Bristol

107. Which famous landmark is visible from space?

    A. The Great Wall of China
    B. Taj Mahal
    C. The Great Pyramids at Giza
    D. Taipei 101

108. Madison Square Garden is home to which NBA team?

    A. New York Knicks
    B. Brooklyn Nets
    C. Philadelphia 76ers
    D. Boston Celtics

109. In what year was the first iPhone released?

    A. 2005
    B. 2007
    C. 2009
    D. 2010

110. Who was the first Roman emperor?

    A. Caesar
    B. Augustus
    C. Marius
    D. Cicero

111. Who invented the rocking chair?

    A. Thomas Edison
    B. Nikola Tesla
    C. Thomas Jefferson
    D. Benjamin Franklin

112. How would you write the number 5 in binary code?

    A. 1
    B. 11
    C. 101
    D. 111

113. Europe is separated from Africa by which sea?

    A. Mediterranean Sea
    B. Black Sea
    C. Red Sea
    D. Balkan Sea

114. Who created the animated series Futurama?

    A. Homer Groening
    B. John Groening
    C. Adam Groening
    D. Matt Groening

115. Which is the main substance used to make a crayon?

    A. Dye
    B. Wax
    C. Plastic
    D. Chalk

116. St. Louis Rams hold the distinction of being the first team to:

    A. Put their logo on their helmets
    B. Not have a mascot
    C. Have a mascot
    D. Put up a team logo

117. Which among these countries do NOT use Euro as its currency?

    A. Belgium

    B. Austria

    C. Monaco

    D. Ukraine

118. Pol Pot ruled which country from 1975-1979?

    A. India

    B. China

    C. Cambodia

    D. Vietnam

119. Which kind of bulbs were once exchanged as a form of currency?

    A. Daffodils

    B. Amaryllis

    C. Tulips

    D. Aliums

120. Who wrote Frankenstein?

    A. Mary Shelley

    B. Percy Shelley

    C. Franklin Stein

    D. Howard Young

121. What is the number one seller at Walmart?

    A. Toilet paper
    B. Bananas
    C. Socks
    D. Greeting Cards

122. What was the first fruit that was eaten on the moon?

    A. Apple
    B. Plum
    C. Melon
    D. Peach

123. The coldest place on Earth is located in which continent?

    A. Antarctica
    B. North America
    C. Asia
    D. South America

124. Which country is NOT part of the Mediterranean?

    A. Italy
    B. Greece
    C. Germany
    D. Spain

125. Who is the youngest player ever to hit 500 home runs?

    A. Gary Sheffield
    B. Alex Rodriguez
    C. Jimmie Foxx
    D. David Ortiz

126. What was Babe Ruth's first name?

    A. George
    B. Gregory
    C. Gerald
    D. Gary

127. What can't a cheetah do that a tiger and a puma can do?

    A. Snarl
    B. Retract its claws
    C. Hibernate
    D. Swim

128. What is the main ingredient of Bombay Duck?

    A. Swan
    B. Chicken
    C. Pork
    D. Fish

129. What type of animal baby is a cria?

    A. camel
    B. crocodile
    C. llama
    D. weasel

130. In Swedish a skvader is a rabbit with what unusual feature?

    A. Wings
    B. Canine teeth
    C. Blue eyes
    D. No tail

131. Which of Shakespeare's plays is the longest?

    A. Macbeth
    B. The Tempest
    C. Hamlet
    D. Taming of the Shrew

132. What country has competitive office chair racing?

    A. Thailand
    B. Japan
    C. Chile
    D. Canada

133. Other than Sculptures what else was Michelangelo known for?

    A. Poetry
    B. music
    C. theatre
    D. dance

134. Which city is the most sung about?

    A. New York
    B. Miami
    C. Los Angeles
    D. London

135. How many time zones does the United States have?

    A. 12
    B. 9
    C. 5
    D. 14

136. Which city was Beethoven born in?

    A. Bonn
    B. Berlin
    C. Munich
    D. Warsaw

137. Coprastastaphobia is the fear of what?

    A. Constipation
    B. Cockroaches
    C. Cobras
    D. Corn

138. Name the team with the most Super Bowl appearances?

    A. Buffalo Bills
    B. New England Patriots
    C. Dallas Cowboys
    D. Pittsburgh Steelers

139. What was the famous Roe vs. Wade case about?

    A. Slavery
    B. drugs
    C. abortion
    D. same-sex marriage

140. Amino acids are the building blocks of which molecules?

    A. carbohydrates
    B. lipids
    C. proteins
    D. sugars

141. Which US state has the highest resident population?

    A. Texas

    B. Ohio

    C. California

    D. Delaware

142. What type of tree grows from an acorn?

    A. elm

    B. fir

    C. maple

    D. oak

143. Who was the first Prime Minister of Canada?

    A. John A. Macdonald

    B. Robert Borden

    C. R. B. Bennett

    D. John Abbott

144. Who signed the Magna Carta?

    A. King George

    B. King William

    C. King John

    D. Queen Victoria

145. Parmesan cheese originated from which country?

   A. France
   B. USA
   C. Belgium
   D. Italy

146. Among land animals what species has the largest eyes?

   A. Ostrich
   B. Lions
   C. Elephants
   D. Komodo Dragons

147. What was Harry Houdini's real name?

   A. Erik Weisz
   B. Aaron Wein
   C. Harry Weisz
   D. Harry Truman

148. Which is the world's highest waterfall?

   A. Kunchikal Falls
   B. Ribbon Fall
   C. Angel Falls
   D. Yosemite Falls

149. What kind of an animal is known as a horned toad?

A. A frog
B. A lizard
C. A beetle
D. A toad

150. Dendrophobia is the fear of what?

A. Flowers
B. Trees
C. The Night Sky
D. Wind

151. Which 1998 Disney film was Lindsay Lohan's film debut?

A. Freaky Friday
B. Parent Trap
C. Mean Girls
D. Just My Luck

152. What are people who love eating ice called?

A. Iconoclasts
B. Aquaphages
C. Pagophagiacs
D. Dontists

153. Which artist painted Guernica?

A. Pablo Picasso
B. Claude Monet
C. Vincent van Gogh
D. Salvador Dali

154. Which Saint banished all snakes from Ireland?

A. Patrick
B. Nicholas
C. Paul
D. Anne

155. It is illegal to do what in the French vineyards?

A. Have a picnic
B. Curse
C. Die
D. Land a flying saucer

156. Where is the Mariana Trench is located?

A. Pacific Ocean
B. Indian Ocean
C. Atlantic Ocean
D. Arctic Ocean

157. Who wrote Catcher in the Rye?

A. George Orwell
B. Truman Capote
C. T.S. Elliot
D. J.D Salinger

158. The One World Trade Center is located in which American city?

A. Los Angeles
B. New York
C. Seattle
D. San Francisco

159. Which is considered the coffee capital of the world?

A. Seoul
B. Wellington
C. Melbourne
D. Vienna

160. What does the Rstand for on the rating of a movie?

A. Registered
B. Restricted
C. Rap
D. Regulated

161. Who was the first person in space?

    A. Neil Armstrong
    B. Yuri Gagarin
    C. Alexei Leonov
    D. Valentina Tereshkova

162. Where would you find the smallest bones in the human body?

    A. ear
    B. finger
    C. spine
    D. toe

163. Lemons originated from which country?

    A. India
    B. USA
    C. Australia
    D. New Zealand

164. Which atmospheric layer is closest to the earth's surface?

    A. exosphere
    B. mesosphere
    C. stratosphere
    D. troposphere

165. What was the bloodiest battle of the American Civil War?

    A. First Battle of Bull Run
    B. Gettysburg
    C. Battle of Shiloh
    D. Second Battle of Bull Run

166. What is the most abundant metal in the Earth's crust?

    A. Iron
    B. Lead
    C. Aluminium
    D. Sodium

167. Where in your body might you find alveoli?

    A. colon
    B. heart
    C. lungs
    D. stomach

168. The kiwi is native to which country?

    A. Australia
    B. Solomon Islands
    C. New Zealand
    D. Fiji

169. How old was King Tut when he died?

    A. 18
    B. 16
    C. 17
    D. 19

170. What is the capital of New Zealand?

    A. Wellington
    B. Auckland
    C. Christchurch
    D. Napier

171. What is the fastest growing body tissue?

    A. bone marrow
    B. fingernails
    C. hair
    D. skin

172. What bird can remember bad memories for up to 5 years?

    A. Kiwis
    B. Parrots
    C. Crows
    D. Sparrows

173. A flamboyance is a group of what animals?

    A. Doves
    B. Dolphins
    C. Geese
    D. Flamingos

174. What country was formerly called Siam?

    A. Laos
    B. Indonesia
    C. Iran
    D. Thailand

175. Who invented scissors?

    A. Hero of Alexander
    B. Leonardo da Vinci
    C. Johannes Guttenberg
    D. Hans Janssen

176. Who wrote To Kill a Mockingbird?

    A. Harper Lee
    B. Margaret Atwood
    C. Jane Austen
    D. Louisa Alcott

177. When did the Cold War end?

    A. 1978
    B. 1989
    C. 1991
    D. 1994

178. How many faces does a dodecahedron have?

    A. 10
    B. 12
    C. 16
    D. 20

179. Which among these countries do NOT border Italy?

    A. France
    B. Vatican City
    C. San Marino
    D. Belgium

180. What does a Scoville unit measure?

    A. Acidity
    B. Aroma
    C. Spiciness
    D. Heat

181. What is the unit of electrical current?

   A. amp
   B. ohm
   C. volt
   D. watt

182. In June in Wyoming it is illegal to take a picture of what?

   A. An elk
   B. A bison
   C. A geyser
   D. A rabbit

183. Which country is the biggest?

   A. India
   B. Japan
   C. Thailand
   D. Singapore

184. Who was the first U.S Secretary of Treasury?

   A. Alexander Hamilton
   B. John Adams
   C. Aaron Burr
   D. Thomas Edison

185. Copper and tin can be combined to make which metal alloy?

   A. brass
   B. bronze
   C. gold
   D. pewter

186. Where is the Masters Tournament always held?

   A. Shinnecock Hills Golf Club
   B. Inverness Club
   C. Baltusrol Golf Club
   D. Augusta National Golf Club

187. Which is the largest living animal on earth?

   A. blue whale
   B. elephant
   C. humpback whale
   D. whale shark

188. What animal cannot stick out their tongue?

   A. Alligators
   B. Crocodiles
   C. Geckos
   D. Anoles

189. In which city is Jim Morrison buried?

   A. London
   B. Paris
   C. New Orleans
   D. Tokyo

190. What is the name of Donald Duck's sister?

   A. Dorathy Duck
   B. Della Duck
   C. Daisy Duck
   D. Daphne Duck

191. Which country has the most mountains?

   A. India
   B. USA
   C. China
   D. Russia

192. What was Hugh Hefner's jet plane named?

   A. Bad Bunny
   B. Pretty Bunny
   C. Big Bunny
   D. Sweet Bunny

193. Which of these elements is not found in ethanol (alcohol)

    A. carbon
    B. hydrogen
    C. nitrogen
    D. oxygen

194. What year did women get the right to vote in the U.S?

    A. 1920
    B. 1919
    C. 1918
    D. 1921

195. Who was monarch after Queen Elizabeth I?

    A. Henry VI
    B. George II
    C. Victoria
    D. James VI

196. How many states are there in the USA?

    A. 60
    B. 50
    C. 32
    D. 49

197. Humans have 7 neck vertebrae. How many do giraffes have?

    A. 4
    B. 7
    C. 10
    D. 14

198. What country did the U.S. buy Alaska from?

    A. Canada
    B. Mexico
    C. England
    D. Russia

199. By which nickname was Evander Holyfield popularly known?

    A. The Mongoose
    B. The Real Deal
    C. Easton Assassin
    D. Evander Holyfield

200. Which ocean is the Bermuda Triangle located?

    A. North Atlantic
    B. Pacific
    C. Indian
    D. Arctic

1. What is the official and current name of Big Ben?

   Elizabeth Tower

2. What did Alexander Fleming famously discover?

   Penicillin

3. Martin Luther sparked which event?

   Protestant Reformation

4. How many countries are in Asia?

   48

5. Where is Angkor Wat located?

   Cambodia

6. What's the most populous city in the United States?

   New York City

7. Who was the longest-serving U.K. Prime Minister?

   Robert Walpole

8. Which dynasty build most of the Great Wall of China?

   Ming

9. What is the function of a xylem in a plant?

Transport of water

10. In 1979 the USSR invaded which country?

Afghanistan

11. What were the earliest forms of contraceptive made from?

Crocodile Dung

12. What is the fastest growing plant on earth?

Bamboo

13. Port-au-Prince is the capital of which country?

Haiti

14. A cross appears in the flags of these countries except?

Spain

15. Which is the largest living lizard on earth?

Komodo dragon

16. Which below sea level mountain is taller than Mt. Everest?

Mauna Kea

17. Yao Ming played for this NBA team:

Houston Rockets

18. What was discovered in the Yukon in 1896?

gold

19. A manatee is also known as what?

Sea cow

20. Which was the first living creature to be sent to space?

Fruit fly

21. What is the main ingredient in falafel?

Chickpea

22. Who said this was their finest hour?

Winston Churchill

23. What is secreted from the lacrimal gland?

Tears

24. What is the name of the book written by Bobby Fischer?

My 60 Memorable Games

25. Dutch people live in which country?

   Netherlands

26. Which among these states is NOT in the East Coast?

   Oregon

27. What is the largest lizard?

   Komodo dragon

28. Mt. Everest is located in which country?

   Nepal

29. What type of music helps plants grow?

   Classical

30. Which element has the symbol Pb?

   Lead

31. Osteoporosis is a disease affecting which part of the body?

   Bones

32. How long was the Vietnam war?

   19 years

33. Which King of England broke apart from the Catholic Church?

Henry VIII

34. What is the fungi Hydnellum peckii also known as?

The bleeding tooth fungus

35. What is the capital of Qatar?

Doha

36. Where was the first tank produced?

England

37. Which of the following pH values indicates an acidic solution?

PH1

38. The Petronas Towers is located in what country?

Malaysia

39. Mount Kilimanjaro is located in which country?

Tanzania

40. The Mayans worshiped which animal as gods?

turkeys

41. Where in your body is your axilla?

   Armpit

42. When a people are frightened their ears produce more of what?

   Earwax

43. Which war did George Orwell fight in?

   the Spanish Civil War

44. What did the first vending machine dispense?

   Holy Water

45. Distance is equal to speed multiplied by what?

   Time

46. What is the only bird known to fly backwards?

   Hummingbird

47. What was Marilyn Monroe's natural hair color?

   Red

48. Where did rap superstar Eminem grow up?

   Detroit

49. Where is the Stone Henge located?

England

50. Caesar salad originated from which country?

Mexico

51. What is dendrochronology?

Tree-ring dating

52. How long can a cockroach survive without its head?

1 week

53. Which of the following numbers is a prime number?

13

54. Where do natural pearls comes from?

Oysters

55. A pangolin is a type of what?

Mammal

56. What is the loudest animal on Earth?

The sperm whale

57. Complete the title of a 1979 number one by Blondie Heart of...

Glass

58. What color does gold leaf appear if you hold it up to the light?

Green

59. How was the Library of Alexandria destroyed?

fire

60. Which US state has the smallest population?

Wyoming

61. Cirque du Soleil started in what country?

Canada

62. Around how many countries have a royal family?

43

63. Power outages in the US are mostly caused by what?

Squirrels

64. What particle in an atom has a positive charge?

Proton

65. Who is the youngest winner in any Grand Slam tournament?

    Martina Hingis

66. If a male donkey is a jack what is the female called?

    Jenny

67. What year did Harriet Tubman escape slavery?

    1849

68. Nepal is located on which continent?

    Asia

69. What is the capital of Germany?

    Berlin

70. What is the only Portuguese-speaking country in the Americas?

    Brazil

71. Which of these is not a type of wild cat?

    Dingo

72. Which country owns the Galapagos Islands?

    Ecuador

73. Which country is predominantly Buddhist?

   Thailand

74. Susan B. Antony was the first woman to be honored in this way?

   currency

75. Who established the 365-day calendar?

   Julius Caesar

76. The video game Happy Feet features what animals?

   Penguins

77. What language has the most words?

   English

78. What is the capital city of Canada's Yukon territory?

   Whitehorse

79. What is the name of the Earth's largest ocean?

   The Pacific Ocean

80. Galileo was the citizen of which country?

   Italy

81. Florence Nightingale aided the sick and wounded during what war?

The Crimean War

82. Where is the Machu Picchu located?

Peru

83. What is the modern name of Saigon?

Ho Chi Minh

84. What is the softest mineral in the world?

Talc

85. Humphrey Bogart won his only Oscar for what motion picture?

The African Queen

86. Which among these records does Magic Johnson hold?

Oldest player to score 40+ points in a game

87. How did Anne Frank receive her diary?

birthday gift

88. Where would you find cellulose?

Plant tissue

89. What is the real first name of Marilyn Monroe?

Norma Jeane

90. In which country is divorce illegal?

Philippines

91. What did Spain introduce to Ireland in the late 1500s?

Potatoes

92. Which country had a personal union with Denmark?

Iceland

93. Which of these animals lays eggs?

Echidna

94. In Roman Myth Mars is the god of what?

war

95. Which is the biggest moon in the solar system?

Ganymede (Jupiter)

96. Who lives in a trash can on Sesame Street?

Oscar

97. Which U.S. President was the first to ride in a Helicopter?

Eisenhower

98. Where did Leonardo da Vinci spend his final years of life?

France

99. Hinduism originated from which country?

Pakistan

100. Who composed the music for Sonic the Hedgehog 3?

Michael Jackson

101. Ferrari is from from which country?

Italy

102. Who gifted the Statue of Liberty to the U.S.?

France

103. NBA basketball legend Kobe Bryant died in:

A Helicopter crash

104. Marilyn Monroe was married to which famous sportsman?

Joe DiMaggio

105. Who was the captain of the Titanic?

Edward Smith

106. Abbey Road is located in which city?

London

107. Which famous landmark is visible from space?

The Great Pyramids at Giza

108. Madison Square Garden is home to which NBA team?

New York Knicks

109. In what year was the first iPhone released?

2007

110. Who was the first Roman emperor?

Augustus

111. Who invented the rocking chair?

Benjamin Franklin

112. How would you write the number 5 in binary code?

101

113. Europe is separated from Africa by which sea?

Mediterranean Sea

114. Who created the animated series Futurama?

Matt Groening

115. Which is the main substance used to make a crayon?

Wax

116. St. Louis Rams hold the distinction of being the first team to:

Put their logo on their helmets

117. Which among these countries do NOT use Euro as its currency?

Ukraine

118. Pol Pot ruled which country from 1975-1979?

Cambodia

119. Which kind of bulbs were once exchanged as a form of currency?

Tulips

120. Who wrote Frankenstein?

Mary Shelley

121. What is the number one seller at Walmart?

Bananas

122. What was the first fruit that was eaten on the moon?

Peach

123. The coldest place on Earth is located in which continent?

Antarctica

124. Which country is NOT part of the Mediterranean?

Germany

125. Who is the youngest player ever to hit 500 home runs?

Alex Rodriguez

126. What was Babe Ruth's first name?

George

127. What can't a cheetah do that a tiger and a puma can do?

Retract its claws

128. What is the main ingredient of Bombay Duck?

Fish

129. What type of animal baby is a cria?

Llama

130. In Swedish a skvader is a rabbit with what unusual feature?

Wings

131. Which of Shakespeare's plays is the longest?

Hamlet

132. What country has competitive office chair racing?

Japan

133. Other than Sculptures what else was Michelangelo known for?

poetry

134. Which city is the most sung about?

New York

135. How many time zones does the United States have?

9

136. Which city was Beethoven born in?

Bonn

137. Coprastastaphobia is the fear of what?

Constipation

138. Name the team with the most Super Bowl appearances?

New England Patriots

139. What was the famous Roe vs. Wade case about?

abortion

140. Amino acids are the building blocks of which molecules?

Proteins

141. Which US state has the highest resident population?

California

142. What type of tree grows from an acorn?

Oak

143. Who was the first Prime Minister of Canada?

John A. Macdonald

144. Who signed the Magna Carta?

King John

145. Parmesan cheese originated from which country?

Italy

146. Among land animals what species has the largest eyes?

Ostrich

147. What was Harry Houdini's real name?

Erik Weisz

148. Which is the world's highest waterfall?

Angel Falls

149. What kind of an animal is known as a horned toad?

A lizard

150. Dendrophobia is the fear of what?

Trees

151. Which 1998 Disney film was Lindsay Lohan's film debut?

Parent Trap

152. What are people who love eating ice called?

Pagophagiacs

153. Which artist painted Guernica?

Pablo Picasso

154. Which Saint banished all snakes from Ireland?

Patrick

155. It is illegal to do what in the French vineyards?

Land a flying saucer

156. Where is the Mariana Trench is located?

Pacific Ocean

157. Who wrote Catcher in the Rye?

J. D. Salinger

158. The One World Trade Center is located in which American city?

New York

159. Which is considered the coffee capital of the world?

Vienna

160. What does the R stand for on the rating of a movie?

Restricted

161. Who was the first person in space?

Yuri Gagarin

162. Where would you find the smallest bones in the human body?

Ear

163. Lemons originated from which country?

India

164. Which atmospheric layer is closest to the earth's surface?

Troposphere

165. What was the bloodiest battle of the American Civil War?

Gettysburg

166. What is the most abundant metal in the Earth's crust?

Aluminium

167. Where in your body might you find alveoli?

Lungs

168. The kiwi is native to which country?

New Zealand

169. How old was King Tut when he died?

19

170. What is the capital of New Zealand?

Wellington

171. What is the fastest growing body tissue?

Bone marrow

172. What bird can remember bad memories for up to 5 years?

Kiwis

173. A flamboyance is a group of what animals?

Flamingos

174. What country was formerly called Siam?

Thailand

175. Who invented scissors?

Leonardo da Vinci

176. Who wrote To Kill a Mockingbird?

Harper lee

177. When did the Cold War end?

1989

178. How many faces does a dodecahedron have?

12

179. Which among these countries do NOT border Italy?

Belgium

180. What does a Scoville unit measure?

Spiciness

181. What is the unit of electrical current?

Amp

182. In June in Wyoming it is illegal to take a picture of what?

A rabbit

183. Which country is the biggest?

India

184. Who was the first U.S Secretary of Treasury?

Alexander Hamilton

185. Copper and tin can be combined to make which metal alloy?

Bronze

186. Where is the Masters Tournament always held?

Augusta National Golf Club

187. Which is the largest living animal on earth?

Blue whale

188. What animal cannot stick out their tongue?

Crocodiles

189. In which city is Jim Morrison buried?

Paris

190. What is the name of Donald Duck's sister?

Della Duck

191. Which country has the most mountains?

USA

192. What was Hugh Hefner's jet plane named?

Big Bunny

193. Which of these elements is not found in ethanol (alcohol)

Nitrogen

194. What year did women get the right to vote in the U.S?

1920

195. Who was monarch after Queen Elizabeth I?

James VI

196. How many states are there in the USA?

50

197. Humans have 7 neck vertebrae. How many do giraffes have?

7

198. What country did the U.S. buy Alaska from?

Russia

199. By which nickname was Evander Holyfield popularly known?

The Real Deal

200. Which ocean is the Bermuda Triangle located?

North Atlantic

SECTION 2

ANSWERS

All Feedback ON AMAZON IS GREATLY APPRECIATED

Made in the USA
Monee, IL
11 March 2021